WHY ARE ANIMALS ORANGE?

Melissa Stewart

Series Literacy Consultant:
Allan A. De Fina, PhD
Dean, College of Education/Professor of Literacy
   Education, New Jersey City University
Past President of the New Jersey Reading Association

Series Science Consultant:
Helen Hess, PhD
Professor of Biology
College of the Atlantic
Bar Harbor, Maine

Contents

Words to Know

attract (uh TRAKT)—To make interested.

blend in—To match; to look the same as.

coral (KOR uhl)—A tiny ocean animal. Some corals live in groups. Others live alone. Some corals are hard. They make up coral reefs.

predator (PREH duh tur)—An animal that hunts and kills other animals for food.

prey (PRAY)—An animal that is hunted by a predator.

survive (sur VYV)—To stay alive.

northern
cardinal

yellow boxfish

A Rainbow of Animals

panther chameleon

poison dart
frog

Go outside and look around. How many kinds of animals do you see? Cats and birds are animals. So are fish and insects.

Animals come in all sizes and shapes. And they come in all the colors of the rainbow.

leaf-mimic katydid

lesser purple
emperor butterfly

Orange Animals Near You

Can you think of some orange animals that live near you? Some insects are orange. So are some birds.

Orange animals live in other parts of the world too. Let's take a look at some of them.

Bengal Tiger

Being orange helps some animals hide. This tiger's orange fur and black stripes make it hard to see. It can sneak through the grass and catch its prey by surprise.

Ambon Shrimp

This little shrimp lives on top of animals called feather stars. It eats their leftover food. The shrimp changes its color to match the animal it is on. It can turn from orange to red, yellow, or white. It can even have spots or stripes.

Coral Grouper

A bright orange fish could really stand out. But not when it swims in front of a bright orange fan coral. Blending in helps animals stay safe. That is why many colorful creatures live on colorful coral reefs.

Scarab Beetle

Some land animals use the same kind of trick. This beetle is hard to see when it rests on an orange flower. That keeps it safe from birds, bats, and other **predators**.

Giant Cuttlefish

This animal lives in the ocean, but it is not a fish. It has more in common with an octopus. Most of the time, its skin is orange. If an enemy gets too close, it can quickly change its color to match the rocks nearby.

Viceroy Butterfly

Some orange animals are easy to spot. Their bright colors send a message. They say, "Stay away!" After just one bite, a hungry bird spits this butterfly out. Yuck! It tastes bad.

Golden Mantella Frog

Most orange frogs taste bad too. This keeps predators away. But this orange frog does *NOT* taste bad. Its color fools predators. They leave the frog alone.

Cock-of-the-Rock

This bird's orange feathers help him attract a mate. They say, "Look at me!" The female's body is not as bright. That helps her hide from predators while she sits on her eggs.

Panther Chameleon

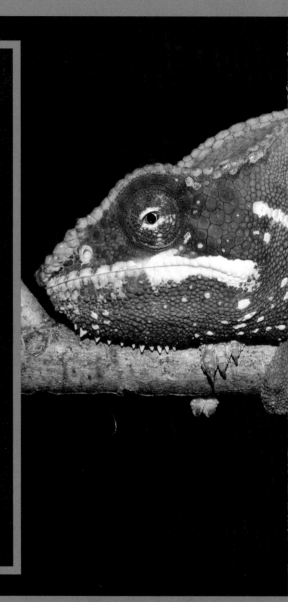

Most of the time, this lizard stays green. That helps it blend in with its forest home. But it can change its color when it wants to send a message. Sometimes it is trying to attract a mate. And sometimes it is telling other lizards to stay away.

Guessing Game

Being orange helps many kinds of animals survive. It helps some animals send a message to mates or predators. It helps other animals hide from their enemies. How do you think being orange helps the animals in these photos?

northern oriole

(See answers on page 32.)

stinkbug

Where Do These Orange

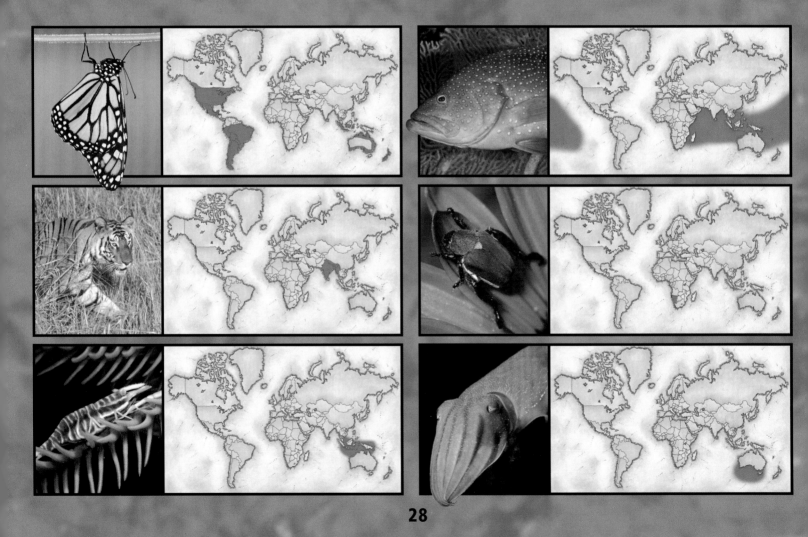

Animals Live?

KEY:
The orange areas on each map below show where that animal lives.

Learn More

Books

Jenkins, Steve. *Living Color*. Boston: Houghton Mifflin, 2007.

Kalman, Bobbie, and John Crossingham. *Camouflage: Changing to Hide*. New York: Crabtree Publishing, 2005.

Stockland, Patricia M. *Red Eyes or Blue Feathers:A Book About Animal Colors*. Minneapolis, Minn.: Picture Window Books, 2005.

Whitehouse, Patricia. *Colors We Eat: Orange Foods*. Chicago: Heinemann, 2004.

Learn More

Index

A attract, 22, 24

C changing color, 10, 16, 24

    coral, 13

E eggs, 22

F feathers, 22

    fur, 9

H hide, 9, 26

M mate, 22, 24, 26

P predators, 15, 21, 22, 26

    prey, 9

S skin, 16

    spots, 10

    stripes, 9, 10

    survive, 26

Enslow Elementary, an imprint of Enslow Publishers, Inc.

Enslow Elementary® is a registered trademark of Enslow Publishers, Inc.

Copyright © 2009 by Melissa Stewart

Library of Congress Cataloging-in-Publication Data

Stewart, Melissa.

   Why are animals orange? / Melissa Stewart.

     p. cm. — (Rainbow of animals)

   Includes bibliographical references.

   Summary: "Uses examples of animals in the wild to explain why some animals are orange"—Provided by publisher.

   ISBN 978-0-7660-3250-7

   1. Animals—Color—Juvenile literature. 2. Orange (Color)—Juvenile literature. I. Title.

QL767.S747 2009

591.47'2—dc22   2008011471

ISBN-10: 0-7660-3250-7

Printed in the United States of America

10 9 8 7 6 5 4 3 2 1

To Our Readers: We have done our best to make sure all Internet Addresses in this book were active and appropriate when we went to press. However, the author and the publisher have no control over and assume no liability for the material available on those Internet sites or on other Web sites they may link to. Any comments or suggestions can be sent by e-mail to comments@enslow.com or to the address on the back cover.

♻ Enslow Publishers, Inc., is committed to printing our books on recycled paper. The paper in every book contains 10% to 30% post-consumer waste (PCW). The cover board on the outside of each book contains 100% PCW. Our goal is to do our part to help young people and the environment too!

Every effort has been made to locate all copyright holders of material used in this book. If any errors or omissions have occurred, corrections will be made in future editions of this book.

All photos by Minden Pictures:
Interior: © Barry Mansell/npl, p. 5 (frog); © Chris Newbert, p. 4 (boxfish); © Frans Lanting, pp. 5 (katydid), 6–7, 22–23, 29 (cock-of-the-rock); © Fred Bavendam, pp. 1 (bottom right), 10–11, 12–13, 16–17, 28 (shrimp, fish, cuttlefish); © Gerry Ellis, pp. 18–19, 29 (butterfly); © Hans Cristoph Kappel/npl, p. 5 (butterfly); © Ingo Arndt, pp. 27, 29 (stinkbug); © Jim Brandenburg, p. 1 (bottom left); © Martin Harvey/Foto Natura, pp. 1 (top right), 20–21, 29 (frog); © Michael & Patricia Fogden, pp. 1 (top left), 14–15, 28 (beetle); © Mitsuaki Iwago, pp. 8–9, 28 (tiger); © Pete Oxford, pp. 4 (chameleon), 24–25, 29 (chameleon); © Rolf Nussbaumer/npl, p. 28 (butterfly); © Tom Vezo, pp. 4 (cardinal), 26, 29 (oriole).
Cover: (clockwise from top left) © Martin Harvey/Foto Natura; © Fred Bavendam; © Jim Brandenburg; © Michael & Patricia Fogden.

Illustration Credits: © 1999, Artville, LLC, pp. 28–29 (maps).

Note to Parents and Teachers: The *Rainbow of Animals* series supports the National Science Education Standards for K–4 science. The Words to Know section introduces subject-specific vocabulary words, including pronunciation and definitions. Early readers may need help with these new words.

Answers to the Guessing Game

The orange belly of a male northern oriole helps it attract a mate.

The bright colors of a stinkbug warn predators to stay away. If an enemy attacks, it will be sorry. The little insect will let out a nasty smell.

Enslow Elementary
an imprint of
Enslow Publishers, Inc.
40 Industrial Road
Box 398
Berkeley Heights, NJ 07922
USA
http://www.enslow.com